The Ultimate Guide To Filmmaking

How To Direct A Movie From Script To Screen Using Latest Techniques

George K.

Table of Contents

Introduction

Chapter 1 – What is Filmmaking?

Chapter 2 – The Development Stage

Chapter 3 – The Pre-Production Stage

Chapter 4 – The Production Stage

Chapter 5 – Post-Production Stage

Chapter 6 – Distribution

Conclusion

Introduction

I want to thank you and congratulate you for purchasing the book, *"The Ultimate Guide to Filmmaking: How to Direct a Movie from Script to Screen Using Latest Techniques"*.

This book contains proven steps and strategies on how to direct a movie effectively. It provides some tips – from writing a script up to the production and distribution of the film.

Filmmaking is an art, but unlike other forms of art, its successful completion requires more than just one person. It only took one Michelangelo to make the Madonna and Child. It only took one Leonardo Da Vinci to make the Last Supper, but the process of filmmaking can never be attributed to just a single person. It involves more people than what you initially thought. These people play crucial roles - starting from scriptwriting to the actual filmmaking process.

Filmmaking is a long process, which requires modifications and adjustments every now and then until the entire team reach their desired output. With that in mind, you can seek the aid of this book if you want to master the art of filmmaking using highly effective tips.

Thanks again for purchasing this book, I hope you enjoy it!

© **Copyright 2014 by George K. - All rights reserved.**

This document is geared towards providing exact and reliable information in regards to the topic and issue covered. The publication is sold with the idea that the publisher is not required to render accounting, officially permitted, or otherwise, qualified services. If advice is necessary, legal or professional, a practiced individual in the profession should be ordered.

- From a Declaration of Principles which was accepted and approved equally by a Committee of the American Bar Association and a Committee of Publishers and Associations.

In no way is it legal to reproduce, duplicate, or transmit any part of this document in either electronic means or in printed format. Recording of this publication is strictly prohibited and any storage of this document is not allowed unless with written permission from the publisher. All rights reserved.

The information provided herein is stated to be truthful and consistent, in that any liability, in terms of inattention or otherwise, by any usage or abuse of any policies, processes, or directions contained within is the solitary and utter responsibility of the recipient reader. Under no circumstances will any legal responsibility or blame be held against the publisher for any reparation, damages, or monetary loss due to the information herein, either directly or indirectly.

Respective authors own all copyrights not held by the publisher.

The information herein is offered for informational purposes solely, and is universal as so. The presentation of the information is without contract or any type of guarantee assurance.

The trademarks that are used are without any consent, and the publication of the trademark is without permission or backing by the trademark owner. All trademarks and brands within this book are for clarifying purposes only and are the owned by the owners themselves, not affiliated with this document.

Chapter 1 – What is Filmmaking?

As mentioned in the first part of this book, filmmaking is an art. Everyone can attest to that fact. It is an art because it requires one to present his creative ideas. The entire process makes it possible for one's creative ideas to come to life. However, please note that while the process may start with the ideas of just one person, its successful completion requires the help of other people. To help you understand the filmmaking process even better, here is a brief description of each of its stages or parts.

1. Development

This is the stage when the creative ideas of a person will start to come to life. This is made possible with the help of the other members of his team. The development stage involves things like writing the script/story, polishing it, and looking for ways to finance the entire project.

2. Pre-Production

The pre-production process takes place when all the needed preparations for the actual filming take place. Among the things that are addressed during this stage are casting, finding the right people to help in the filmmaking process, and selecting the right location.

3. Production

This stage involves the actual filming and recording of the raw elements or scenes of the film.

4. Post-Production

After the raw scenes or elements, like the images, footage, and visual and sound effects are taken, the post-production stage comes next. It involves editing those raw elements and making all the necessary adjustments to create the most desirable output.

5. Distribution

After editing the film and achieving the final output, the distribution process takes place. This is the part wherein you need to distribute the film to various channels and make it reach the target viewers. It also involves handling contracts on how, where, and when the distribution process should take place.

These are just five of the most important parts/stages in the filmmaking process. It often takes months and years to finish a high quality film. However, there is also one film, which was successfully completed in as short as 4 days. This is the Shotgun Garfunkel of South America, which is considered as the fastest film ever created in history. The Thief and the Cobbler, on the other hand, is a British animation film, which took years to complete.

Now that you have an overview of each stage of the filmmaking process, it is time to discuss them in full detail. Continue reading the next chapters of this book as they contain more information about each stage of filmmaking.

Chapter 2 – The Development Stage

The development stage, in the field of filmmaking, is when an idea starts taking its shape. Here are some important points to remember during this stage:

a. Actual events that made an impact on the writers should inspire the generation of the idea. It would be best to write from experience or based on what you know, so you can effectively relay your point to the viewers.

b. Set an inspiring and motivating area for you where you can write down your ideas. Make sure that the area is conducive to writing. It should be free from all forms of destruction. The place should inspire you to write from the heart and weave the best story that you can ever think of.

c. Determine the plot, format and genre of the story before starting to write the first chapter. This is helpful in setting the flow of the story.

The Script

The journey to a thousand miles, they say, begins with a single step. The same concept applies to filmmaking. A great movie starts with one creative idea or unique story. Scriptwriting, therefore, is the most important part of filmmaking.

A writer can take a few pathways in his journey to writing the best script. You may opt to write your own script, if you are passionate in this area, or hire a more experienced scriptwriter to create the story for you.

I. Writing an Original Script

If you decide to write your own script, then make sure that you have a solid idea. You can do so by learning the major motivating factor for writing or creating the film first. Are you planning to create a movie for profit, or just because it is your passion? Your answer to this question will help you develop the flow of the story.

If you intend to produce a film for the purpose of earning profit, then make sure that your story appeals to your target audience. Know the type of audience that you would like to reach then weave your story in such a way that you can tap their interest. To gain profit, your ticket sales should be more than enough to cover the cost of filming.

Most commercialized films are based on scripts that specifically address the concern of a target audience. If you want to create a film for children, then your script should be written in a fun, engaging and animated way to win their attention.

However, if you are planning to create a film, not for profit, but to satisfy your love and passion for this form of art, then you can do anything that you want with it. Just make sure that it is still engaging, since it is more satisfying to know that you were able to satisfy a lot of people because of your passion and talent in this field.

Getting someone to produce your script is essential; hence, it is essential to balance the two options – writing a script from your heart or based on your passion and ensuring that it will sell. Note that the main goal of filmmaking is to earn profit. Producers choose stories that sell.

The industry formula, which is considered as the standard formula in the filmmaking process, involves a defined genre, a structure with 3 acts, salable actors and top of the line production. While this can cost you money, your chances of earning profit right after the film is released to the public are higher.

If you are still a beginner who wants to hone your scriptwriting and filmmaking talent, then creating a short script or film is the best way to start. You are still on the stage of honing your skills in this field, so it would be unwise to jump on risky projects immediately. However, you can't expect producers and executives to finance your short film at first, so be prepared to cut corners and lose some money along the process.

Eventually, you'll master the art of scriptwriting and filmmaking, which will be a huge help in encouraging producers to finance your projects.

Write from the Heart

Like what most writers say, it is important to write from the heart. Seek inspiration from your own experiences and the experiences of others. Also, it would be best to write about something that you are knowledgeable about, so your story will flow smoothly without any loose ends.

Write about something you have seen with your own two eyes. Inspiration is everywhere. Be a wide reader and a keen observer. Your next story may be about something you have read in today's newspaper, or something you've heard on the radio. You can write about anything, which captures your interest because there is a great chance that your target audience will also love it.

Write about something you have experienced yourself. Draw inspiration from your life. You can actually create a story from your current situation. It could be based from your childhood memories or from a conversation that you just had with someone in the office. Weaving a story out of your personal experiences will most likely create a solid material for a film because it will surely come from your heart.

Keeping a journal is crucial if you want to write from the heart and be more effective in the field of scriptwriting. You can use your journal to record relevant experiences during the day. This will prevent you from forgetting a creative idea, which just pops on your mind.

Learning more about history is also a great way to write a solid script. Start learning from the lives of famous people, dictators, emperors and other important personalities in history. Who knows, you will gain inspiration from their own stories and create a story that will appeal to the masses?

When writing a script, avoid copying someone else's ideas. Be original to prevent yourself from facing legal issues just because you've copied the work of others. Don't forget to take a break from time to time. Don't write when you are already too tired because it will only cause you to create an awful story. Relax and don't pressure yourself.

Clear your mind for a few minutes if you experience writer's block, instead of forcing yourself to finish it. A few minutes of relaxation is often enough to bring back your momentum, allowing you to continue weaving an inspiring story.

II. Use Someone Else's Material

You can also create a film using a script that has already been written by someone else. You can even produce a new script out of an existing book, short story or poem. However, it is important to get an option to prevent yourself from violating copyright laws.

An option is basically a lease, which gives a producer the permission to use an existing material and adapt or turn it into a movie. This may cost more than creating an original script, but it somehow guarantees profit. For example, the producers of Harry Potter did not need to make a new story, but optioned to adapt J.K Rowling's book. This is because they know that the story sells, therefore, there is also a great chance for the movie to become profitable.

III. Work with another Writer

Working with another writer is also a great idea. This makes it easier to brainstorm ideas and provide immediate feedback. Make sure, however, that you work with a writer who has the same vision as yours. You have to agree on the concept or story for more effective collaboration. When searching for a writer whom you can work with, make sure to look for the following:

1. Writing Sample

Always ask for a writing sample. This will give you an idea about his writing style. You can ask him to provide you with a script that he has previously written. Try reading the first 20 pages, so you'll know if his writing style fits yours. This is also an effective way to gauge the ability of the writer to engage his audience.

2. Know your Weaknesses

It is also crucial to know and accept your weaknesses, so you can find someone who can fill in those shortcomings. Know the specific area in the field of scriptwriting where you usually fail. Among the most important areas of scriptwriting are structure, characterization and dialogue. If you are weak in one of these areas, then consider hiring a writer who is skillful in it, so you can complement each other.

3. Specialization

Make sure that your potential partner loves the story and genre. For instance, if you are after creating a romantic comedy script, then a writer who is also interested in this genre is the best person to hire.

4. Work Commitment

You will have a hard time finishing a script if you work with a writer who can't seem to commit fully to the entire project. Find out if he has other obligations that have the potential of interfering with project completion. Work with someone who can fully commit to the project. If possible, let him sign an agreement, which requires him to give his full commitment on what you will be working on.

5. Terms and Conditions

It is advisable to get a signed agreement of the project details. Before starting to collaborate with another writer, discuss the terms and conditions of the project. Include these relevant details in the agreement. This is crucial in ensuring that all the important details are clearly conveyed.

Story Structure

A house needs a good foundation. The same goes with scriptwriting. Creating a solid foundation helps in narrowing down the focus of the story and keeping its message intact. To ensure that your script will have a solid structure, you need to consider the following things:

1. Fiction or True Story

The first option you need to consider is whether your story will be based on fiction or on a true story. Fictional stories have made-up characters who live in made-up worlds or situations. These stories are mainly based on imagination than fact, thereby allowing a writer to go outside of his real world.

True stories, as the name suggests, are based on the real stories and experiences of actual people. Some examples of non-fiction films are biographies and documentaries. If you choose this option, then note that you may need to secure rights for adaptation.

2. Genre

Distributors traditionally favor materials that they can easily pitch to potential buyers, so it is crucial for your script to be easily identified within a specific type or genre. The most common types of genre are the following:

- Romantic comedy
- Drama
- Romance
- Action
- Crime
- Comedy
- Fantasy
- Family
- Western
- Thriller
- Musical
- Science Fiction
- War
- Horror

3. Format

You can also format your script based on your intended purpose. Here are the main formats where you can base your script on:

a. Animation

If you decide to create a script for an animated film, then take note that it may consume a lot of your time. It is advisable to write the script yourself, if you have the skills for it, so you can limit the amount of money that you'll invest on it. Note that animation films often come with high production and development costs, so it would be best to know where you can save.

b. Feature Films

Feature films often involve a 90-minute narrative story. This is probably the riskiest production because it is quite expensive and investments are rarely recouped by finances.

c. Documentaries

This type of format aims to study or explore a particular subject matter, like a belief or a specific occurrence. It also usually ends with a conclusion about the chosen topic. This format usually requires you to do extensive investigation, making it time-consuming to produce.

d. Short Films

These are ideally 20 minutes in length

or less, making them effective in selling a writer's skills. Filmmakers usually make short films to get recognized in the industry. This format, despite being short, is usually enough to showcase the skills of a scriptwriter and filmmaker, as well as his ability to capture the interest of his target audience.

4. Plot

Stories always come with a plot with three distinct parts called acts.

a. Act 1

This is the first 30 minutes of a film, which works by establishing the setting of the story. In this part, the main characters are introduced to the audience. Basically, this part answers the following questions:

- Who the characters are?

- Where the story revolves around?

- Where the story will take place?

- What is the conflict?

- What causes the conflict?

b. Act 2

Basically, this is the part when the conflict is clearly introduced. It usually runs starting from the 30-minute to the 90-minute period. An important part of this act is the turning point because this is when you will notice the twist of the story.

c. Act 3

Usually taking place in the last 30 minutes of the film, this is when the main character will be forced to resolve the conflict. It ends with the conclusion of the story and the conflict resolution. The main character may either turn for the worse or get better in this part.

5. Characters

The characters make the story, so it is crucial to write characters whom the audience can relate to. Develop each character's background in such a way that they become more realistic and relatable. Here are some effective tips in creating your characters:

a. Base the characters on people you actually know. It will be easier for you to create a dialogue if you have a specific character in mind.

b. Create interesting names. You can use a book of baby names or search names on the internet. Online name generators are also currently available, making it easier for you to generate unique names. Make sure to choose names for your characters that are not only unique, but are also easy to remember.

c. Make the characters interesting by describing their strengths and their weaknesses. Give the audience an idea regarding the personality of a character by showing them how he will react in various situations.

Character Categories

1. Protagonist

The protagonist is the main character of the story. In most cases, a story focuses on his life lessons, although there are instances when his story is conveyed to the audience based on another person's perspective.

2. Antagonist

This is literary the protagonist's opposite character. The antagonist presents challenges that the protagonist should overcome. Though not necessarily a bad character, the antagonist just has his own goals that are extremely different from that of the protagonist.

3. Supporting Characters

These characters are written to back up either the protagonist or the antagonist. They usually have similar objectives with the main characters.

6. Dialogue

This is probably the most difficult element in the field of scriptwriting. It reflects the quality of characterization in the story, so you need to plan it carefully. One tip in creating dialogue is to ensure that it is original by avoiding overused words or clichés. It is also advisable to develop each character first. This is crucial in ensuring that they don't sound the same or that they don't have similar personalities. Determine how you want each of your characters to think, act and say, as this is the key to creating solid and strong dialogue.

Staying true to your character's heritage is also crucial in creating the most memorable dialogues. For instance, if you are planning to write about a British character, then make sure that you know exactly how they pronounce certain words or phrases. You need to conduct extensive research to make your dialogues sound accurate.

Finish your Script

Here are some important things to remember when finishing your script:

- Check your grammar and proofread your work. If you want production companies to take your script seriously, hand them an error-free script.

- Don't just photocopy your material. Submit clean copies of your screenplay and print a fresh batch whenever you plan to present it to producers.

- Follow the standard format. Use 12-point Courier font written on an 8.5 x 11 bond paper. Companies receive hundreds of screenplays a day and usually discard scripts that don't follow industry standards.

- Protect your script by creating a copyright. This process may involve a nominal fee, but is valuable in proving a script's authenticity.

Chapter 3 – The Pre-Production Stage

The pre-production stage starts right after you're done with the script. It involves the following vital parts:

- **Script breakdown**

    This first step in pre-production is crucial in coming up with solid storyboards. It basically involves analyzing the script, making it possible to budget the production and schedule the shoot.

    The storyboard is composed of sketches that show parts of the script. This may include information about panning and zooming a particular frame shot. It helps save time because it allows you to address potential problems in shooting before they occur.

- **Budget calculation**

    It is crucial to create a budget, so you can effectively plan for production expenditures. Every part of the production process involves expenses. Consider the location, storyboard, cast and crew when creating the film's budget.

Knowledge in the latest version of MS Excel and other applications like QuickBooks is helpful in this process.

- **Financing**

   After creating the budget, the next step is to secure financing. This is possible by presenting your screenplay to producers. You can also call companies and ask for sponsorships in exchange for some airtime in the film. Do you notice some movies that only showcase a particular brand of cellphone? That's an example of a company sponsoring a film.

- **Location scouting**

   The location depends on the story and your budget. If you have a limited budget, then staying in just one location is advisable. However, if you are willing to spend more for the film, then you have to determine the size of the project to find the best location for it. Just make sure to get all the necessary permits for shooting a film, since some states, like Los Angeles, take this matter seriously.

- **Casting**

    Casting should be based on the characters of your story. Some opt to write a character based on a particular actor. However, if you already have a finished script, it would be best to hold auditions to find an actor, who perfectly fits a specific character.

- **Crew and equipment**

    Make sure that you are working with a knowledgeable crew to prevent any problems during the filming process. Also, gather and use the latest film equipment. It is best to go digital because it is cheaper to edit raw scenes digitally.

- **Scheduling of shoots**

    Your entire team should agree to show up on specific shooting schedules before you start filming. Be firm on the schedule to prevent issues on the date and time of access, staging, power usage, ingress and egress of equipment.

The pre-production stage also requires the help of the following, so make sure that you have them in your team:

1. Director

The director is responsible in directing how the story will appear on screen. He is tasked to formulate the best creative and acting decisions necessary in producing a high quality film.

2. Assistant Director

He is responsible for the schedule and logistics of the shooting production.

3. Production Designer

He needs to work with the Art Director and create the visual concept of the entire film.

4. Art Director

He is responsible in coordinating with the art department. He is also tasked to gather the necessary costumes and props.

5. Casting Director

His role is to find the actors who perfectly fit the characters of the film. The casting director schedules actor auditions and coordinate the activities of the chosen actors.

6. Director of Photography

He is responsible in ensuring that the cinematography is at its best. He also needs to address all photography issues linked to filmmaking.

7. Director of Audiography

The audiographer supervises all the sounds needed in the film. Other names used to refer to this vital position are sound designer and supervising sound editor.

The pre-production stage is when you should gather all the necessary tools and equipment for filming. This is crucial in keeping the entire filmmaking process more organized.

Chapter 4 – The Production Stage

The production stage is when all the shooting and filming take place. This stage records all the raw footages. If you want to produce the most captivating film, then the following shooting techniques can help you out during the production stage:

1. Over-the-shoulder Shot

This requires an out-of-focus shot of the actor's shoulder, emphasizing a different situation, which happens somewhere else. On a narrative perspective, you can use this technique to create a sense of intimacy in a scene. It is also an effective tool if you want to communicate the story.

2. Tilt Shot

This shot requires you to tilt the camera up or down to emphasize a particular scene. It is particularly helpful if you want to relay the message to the audience that a particular character is sizing up the character of someone else.

3. Panning Shot

This works like a tilt shot, but done horizontally. This works in drawing the attention of the audience to the story.

4. Zoom Shot

This can produce cool shots, if done correctly. The shots somehow give creepy effects to certain scenes. The best examples of zoom shots are those used in the movies Gladiator and Hannibal.

Production Tips

1. Some ideas don't come as expected. There are also ideas that require a huge amount of money. If you don't have enough budget to achieve what you have envisioned for your film, learn to adapt. In this case, you only have two options - get a financier or find other affordable ways to turn your vision into reality.

2. Always rehearse your blocking. This is crucial in acquainting the actors with the scene, allowing them to move freely and be more comfortable with their individual characters once the actual filming starts.

3. Be flexible to change. Note that there are instances when you need to make adjustments or changes on the original plan. If the change or adjustment is necessary to produce a better film, then be willing to adapt.

4. Wear comfortable outfit. Wear clothes that make you feel comfortable since you'll most likely work on the film for at least twelve hours a day.

5. Take care of your crew. Provide them with adequate food and water. This will inspire them to continue working and produce the best film. Also, give them a break from time to time. Avoid forcing them to work if you noticed that they are already too exhausted.

Coordinate with the finance department. This will ensure that all your expenses will be accounted for. There are minimal expenses that can run over a long period of time, like foods and utilities. Keep track of these expenses to keep the production process running smoothly.

Chapter 5 – Post-Production Stage

This stage is essential because this is where you'll need to analyze all the scenes that you've taken and edit them. The good news is that you can now take advantage of the many editing software available. If you have a limited budget, then you can take advantage of online software that can do the job for minimal cost.

One of the most important things to do in this stage is to ensure that all footages and pictures are sequenced properly. You will also need to sync the audio to the film. If you are planning to use online software, however, avoid uploading the entire film online. This may cause it to leak online, causing you to lose profit.

Linear Editing vs. Non-Linear Editing

Linear editing is a technique, which arranges shots in a sequential order. This is a great editing technique, but note that you'll need to do the entire process again, if you plan to put a specific scene in a different position. This makes it a bit time-consuming. Non-linear editing, on the other hand, makes it possible for you to place each scene in various orders.

This makes it easier and faster for you to edit your shots.

Soundtrack

The post-production stage is the perfect time to add sounds to your film. Ensure that you choose the most appropriate soundtrack for the film. It should be able to build the mood of a specific scene. Note that there are moviegoers out there who are enticed to watch a movie because of the soundtrack. Here are some tips that will help you pick the best soundtrack or background music for your film:

1. Get the rights to the music you plan to use. This is the first thing you have to address if you decide to use the music from other artists. Have a signed agreement that you'll be using the music for the movie. This can help you in times of dispute.

2. Sometimes, less is more. Study each scene carefully and determine whether it requires a background music. Note that there are times when music is no longer necessary to build up the mood of a scene.

3. Avoid using a musical score, which has

already become famous because it is featured in another film. If the viewers realize where the music originally came from, you'll have a hard time relaying the message of your own movie to them.

Chapter 6 – Distribution

Now we are on the last stage of the filmmaking process – the distribution. This involves finally releasing the movies to the cinemas. It also involves directly selling the films to consumers in the form of DVDs, VCDs and the like. To distribute your films effectively, use the following tips:

1. Take advantage of press releases and launch parties – In this case, it is advisable to create banners or previews that will stir the curiosity of potential viewers. Some film distributors opt to launch their films in a particular country. This is a great technique for huge movies because it guarantees international success, which can bring in huge amount of income.

2. Set a movie premiere in a country where you made a particular shot, preferably the most memorable and significant ones in the entire film. Aside from increasing the value of the movie, it can also motivate international viewers to take it seriously.

3. Opt for theatrical release. These days, releasing your film on cinemas may cost a fortune. There are many costs involved, like advertising and press release. The cinemas where you intend to show your film will also get a cut from your income. With a theatrical release, distributors will have the opportunity to offset potential theater losses with the cross-collateralization clause stated in the contract. Releasing your film in theater can also increase the perceived value of any film.

4. Network your production. The film industry is huge and greatly requires excellent skills and knowledge. To earn profit in the filmmaking industry, it is advisable to learn the power of networking. Network with people who have the same interests as you and who can help bring the best out of your film.

5. Distribute your film through various online companies. This is helpful in reaching a wider range of consumers. For example, you can distribute your film through iTunes. This can help distribute your film because it can connect to millions of iTunes users. Even if you don't release your film on various countries, you can still expect it to reach the international market with the help of these online companies.

Note, however, that selling your medium through iTunes may mean selling your film for a much cheaper price. Avoid letting this issue stop you, however, because even if the selling price is low, the number of possible viewers is limitless, making it more profitable than conventional distribution channels.

Just what like this book has extensively discussed, the filmmaking process involves different stages - development, pre-production, production, post-production and distribution stages. Avoid skipping one stage. Note that skipping just one step may ruin your entire film. All the stages are crucial in ensuring that you'll produce a high quality film, which your target audience will love.

Conclusion

Thank you again for purchasing this book!

I hope this book was able to help you to help you find out more information about filmmaking.

Now, you have learned the basics about filmmaking. The next step is to go out there and try to put whatever you have just read into practice. Who knows? You might be the next Steven Spielberg if you start your craft now.

Finally, if you enjoyed this book, then I'd like to ask you for a favor, would you be kind enough to leave a review for this book on Amazon? It'd be greatly appreciated!

Thank you and good luck!

Printed in Great Britain
by Amazon